CAREERS WITH THEME PARKS

DESIGN AND MANAGEMENT

THE MODERN THEME PARK BUSINESS is a globe-spanning, multibillion-dollar extravaganza that relies upon the efforts of engineers, performers, painters, designers, singers, comedians, architects, dancers, writers and every kind of corporate professional imaginable, from accountants to lawyers to marketing pros. In fact, few industries rely on as many different career skill sets as the theme park industry. The magic does not happen by accident.

Americans spend about $25 billion a year on visiting theme parks in the United States. The Disney parks alone receive almost 20 million visitors per year. For many families, packing the car or getting on a plane to spend a week or so on a theme-park vacation is an annual ritual cherished by children and parents alike. In fact, adults outnumber children at Disneyland by about two to one.

A growing economy in the United States and around the world has pumped up demand for theme parks. Theme parks spend around $10 billion on new construction in the United States every year, and that does not count additional spending around the world, often by American companies. While it is true that the theme park business is sensitive to economic downturns, it always bounces back. Having fun is a part of life, and people are happy to spend money on it. There may be a place in this fascinating business for you.

WHAT YOU CAN DO NOW

YOU CAN GET STARTED ON YOUR CAREER in the theme park business right now. Go to as many theme parks as you can and try to figure out what makes them tick. This will not be too hard to do. It will cost some money, to be sure, but the information you discover may be very useful in your career search. Do extensive research in the field. Most theme parks are divided into multiple themes, with each part of the park offering a different experience. Themes are supported by the designed environments, like the architecture of the buildings in a particular area, the costumes worn by cast members, and the topics or look of individual attractions. In your visits, consider which parks do the best job of carrying out their themes? How do they do it? Which parks come up short? How is the food? Are there creative cuisine options or just burgers and hotdogs? Not all theme parks are created equal. Which ones do you like best, and why?

Theme parks are always hiring young people for part-time positions as cast members in their parks. The biggest parks employ thousands of people in flexible, part-time positions ranging from attraction operators, to foodservice professionals, to singers and dancers. If there is a theme park near you, find out what it takes to land a job. You will learn just by working in a theme park, even if you take whatever job is available. In northern climes most theme parks are only open during the summer, but in the southern part of the country they are mostly open year-round. If you do not have access to a major theme park, you can seek out a similar job in a shopping mall, themed restaurant, park district, or tourist attraction. Any job that gives you a good grounding in customer service will be helpful to your career.

Theme parks have legions of fans. Fans do things like build internet blogs with up-to-the-minute news and gossip from their favorites. Look into these sites:

- www.themeparkinsider.com
- www.micechat.com
- www.orlandoparksnews.com
- www.coaster101.com
- www.disneyfoodblog.com

HISTORY OF THE CAREER

MODERN THEME PARKS ARE THE CULMINATION of hundreds of years of innovation. They have been inspired by cities, parks, museums, playgrounds and even rural markets. People have always treasured special places where they can go to have fun, socialize and generally forget their cares, even if only for a little while.

Medieval European villages were generally laid out around a central plaza or square that served several important functions. First and foremost, these open spaces were used to host markets and conduct the commerce that kept village residents working and prosperous. They could also be used for official events like parades and speeches. In-between scheduled events they were the places to see and be seen, to meet with friends and neighbors, and to have fun. Inns and pubs grew up around squares, traveling minstrels and performers passed through, and everybody in town knew that the square was the place to go for holidays and festivals.

Market squares inspired the first European pleasure

gardens, spaces devoted exclusively to amusements. Many pleasure gardens had entrance fees that limited their appeal only to prosperous citizens, but for the price of admission these lucky folks could enjoy attractions like menageries of exotic animals, acrobats and jugglers, elaborate gardens and even fireworks displays. Like market squares, pleasure gardens provided a venue for troupes of traveling performers.

The first pleasure gardens that grew into actual theme parks were both founded in Denmark, and both are still open and operating. Founded in 1583 near Klampenborg, Denmark, Dyrehavsbakken – commonly known simply as Bakken – grew up around a natural spring north of the capital, Copenhagen that was already popular with city dwellers because the water was so much cleaner than the water in the city. In 1843 entrepreneur Georg Carstensen opened the Tivoli Gardens pleasure garden on 15 acres in Copenhagen proper. Both parks now attract millions of guests each year and are home to roller coasters and other modern rides.

The next idea in the development of theme parks was the dawn of the world's fair. The first world's fair was held in London in 1851 in an enormous glass building known as the Crystal Palace. The fair set the standard for fairs to come by inviting countries from around the world to set up pavilions to showcase their arts, culture and technology. World's fairs have been held in cities around the world ever since, typically staged in temporary buildings for a year or so and leaving behind a relic or two for future generations. Chicago's Museum of Science and Industry was originally the Palace des Beaux Arts (Palace of Fine Arts) for the 1893 Colombian Exposition, and the Eiffel Tower in Paris was the symbol of the Exposition Universelle de 1889.

In the United States pleasure gardens were known as amusement parks. The first amusement park in the United

States grew out of Coney Island in Brooklyn, New York. A simple seaside beach resort founded in 1829, Coney Island grew into a sophisticated amusement park with modern rides and attractions along the waterfront. In 1895 Sea Lion Park became a standalone amusement park with an entrance fee.

American amusement parks of the early 20th century were generally rough, unsavory places not fit for family entertainment, at least not after dark. Most cities did not even have a permanent amusement park, but hosted traveling carnivals a few times a year. Carnies, as they were known, often featured bawdy amusements like freak shows and strippers, and were usually forced to set up on the edge of town to limit their malign influence.

Filmmaker Walt Disney was one of the many parents who thought that amusement parks would make great family destinations if only they were clean and professionally run. After World War II, Disney went on a tour of Europe to renegotiate movie distribution contracts disrupted by the war. He brought his family with him to see the sights. Disney was especially impressed by Tivoli Gardens, which was clean, safe, and lively and run by courteous, professional people. Upon returning to his studio in California, he began to toy with the idea of a small amusement park on a vacant lot across the street. The more he thought about it, the bigger the idea became. Eventually he struck a deal with the ABC television network to create a weekly television series that would show Disney programs and keep audiences updated on the progress of his newest venture: Disneyland.

Opened on July 17, 1955 Disneyland was an instant hit. People came from around the world to visit the new park, quickly making Disneyland one of the world's most famous destinations. With Disneyland, Walt Disney also created the template for every theme park that has come since. For starters, he coined the phrase "theme park" to reflect the fact that Disneyland was divided into five different areas with distinct themes: Main Street USA, Frontierland, Adventureland, Tomorrowland and Fantasyland. Each area was home to distinctive architecture, themed attractions and restaurants. Themes were extended to details like railings and fences, benches and tables, and the costumes worn by cast members. Disney also established the language of theme parks, seeing employees as members of a giant cast assembled on a set where customers, known as guests, could imagine themselves in a magical world. He even insisted that Disneyland be surrounded by a berm high enough to block out views of the outside world. Nothing could interfere with the themes.

Disneyland created a new business model that has been adopted by zoos, museums and specialized themed attractions like Sea World and Disney's Animal Kingdom. Principles articulated in theme park design, like forced perspective and laying out attractions with the goal of keeping people moving, have been adopted by shopping malls and city planners. Traditional downtowns once left to ruin when they could not compete with big-box retailers have been revitalized by the efforts of community volunteers inspired by Main Street USA and the Main Street America program run by the National Trust for Historic Preservation. Look around your college campus. Do you see gathering areas, cafes and coffee shops? Ample parking hidden away from view? Complex landscaping and interesting architecture? The medieval market square never went away – it has been reinterpreted, dressed up and made better than ever.

WHERE YOU WILL WORK

THERE ARE THEME PARKS AND THEMED entertainment venues throughout the United States. You ought to be able to start your career just about anywhere. Two regions, however, stand out: Southern California and Central Florida. If you are serious about a career in theme park design and management, you should set your sights on spending a few years in one of these places.

Most major metropolitan areas are home to at least one theme park. Six Flags owns and operates 13 theme parks across the United States, in places like Gurnee, Illinois. (between Chicago and Milwaukee); Austell, Georgia (near Atlanta); Oklahoma City; Eureka, Missouri (near St. Louis); and Largo, Maryland (near Washington, DC). Cedar Fair owns another dozen theme parks around the country, in locations like Muskegon, Michigan; Shakopee, Minnesota (near Minneapolis); and Kansas City, Missouri. Check out their websites for the locations of all of their parks. There are also numerous independent theme parks, like Hersheypark, in Hershey, Pennsylvania and Canobie Lake Park, in Salem, New Hampshire.

Although there are plenty of top-notch theme parks to be found around the country, Southern California and Central Florida are the most popular destinations. Both areas are home to several major parks and, more importantly, to the behind-the-scenes businesses that make theme parks go. Southern California is home to Disneyland, Disney's California Adventure, Knotted's Berry Farm, Six Flags Magic Mountain, Sea World, Universal Studios, Legoland California, Belmont Park, Pacific Park, and dozens of themed attractions that are not traditional theme parks, like the San Diego Zoo's Safari Park and a dozen or so water parks. Central Florida is dominated by

Disney and Universal theme parks, with the giant Walt Disney World Resort offering the Magic Kingdom, Epcot Center, Disney's Hollywood Studios and Disney's Animal Kingdom; and Universal's somewhat smaller resort featuring Universal Studios Florida and Universal's Islands of Adventure. Orlando is also home to a Sea World Park, a Legoland park and more themed water parks, restaurants, museums and miniature golf courses than anywhere in the country. Southern California and Central Florida are also home to many of the businesses behind the scenes, including engineering and architectural firms specializing in theme parks, and the headquarters of Disney and Universal. These companies often branch out beyond theme parks. The United States Navy maintains an office in Orlando because the experts who create simulation technology for use in theme park attractions are the same experts who create simulators for military purposes like pilot training. The Navy even hired experts from the theme park business to build a replica ship to use for training purposes in Navy boot camp.

Keep in mind that there are many other businesses that are not exactly theme parks but require many of the same career skills, like zoos, aquariums, planetariums, museums, parks, sports stadia and even golf courses and shopping malls.

DESCRIPTION OF WORK DUTIES

Attractions Host

Almost everybody in the theme park business started as an attractions host. The smiling faces who have the most contact with the guests, attractions hosts make everything go. They push the buttons, load the cars, and tell guests to keep their hands and arms inside the ride vehicle at all times. For many guests, attractions hosts are the only cast members with whom they have any interaction.

Attractions hosts are what customer-service businesses call "front-line" workers. They are the face of the company and have the most contact with the customers. All theme park companies give their attractions hosts rigorous training in customer service before sending them out among the guests. Training typically lasts anywhere from a full week, usually followed by a few weeks of probationary supervision on the job. Not everybody is cut out for customer service. It is hard to remember that the customer is always right even when some customers are plainly wrong. It is even harder on a busy summer day when the park is packed shoulder-to-shoulder, it is 95 in the shade, and a popular ride has broken down, or even worse, a child has been shaken up by a scarey ride and is crying. Attractions hosts need nerves of steel and the patience of a saint.

They also need to be experts in their little corner of the park. Attractions hosts typically do a morning walk-through of their attraction, checking for problems and making sure everything is working as it should. Maintenance engineers also conduct routine periodic inspections, but it is attractions hosts who are on the spot all day, every day, and have to know what to keep an eye on. A little shimmy on a roller coaster track may not be a big deal if it is fixed quickly, but it could become a serious safety hazard if left unattended for too long. Attractions hosts are the first line of defense against mechanical failures.

Attractions hosts also have to be on the lookout for problems with guests. People often pass out on very hot days, for example, and require medical attention. Attractions hosts must know how to call for emergency help and keep guests comfortable while they wait. Hosts must also be on the lookout for guests with malicious intent. Sometimes guests get angry when they have to wait in line longer than expected, or when something does not go their way. Attractions hosts have to know how to deal with them to defuse any problematic situation.

Do not try to avoid a hitch as an attractions host, even if you are a recent college graduate and think you should be starting at a high employment level. You will learn most of what you really need to know about the theme park business as an attractions host.

Area Manager

Area managers – the title may be different from one employer to the next – are supervisors in charge of all the attractions in a particular area. An area could consist of a small cluster of attractions that share a common building or platform, or an entire themed land. There may be several tiers of area managers, depending upon the park.

Look at photos of theme parks in satellite imagery in an online mapping application. You will see that there are relatively few large buildings in most theme parks. Those large buildings house multiple attractions, restaurants and shops. From eye level they look like separate structures but they often share many backstage facilities. Area managers take charge of these facilities, supervising and scheduling the attractions hosts within them. They work closely with lead attractions hosts at each attraction to solve employee problems, ensure proper scheduling, and report issues to maintenance teams.

Area managers in charge of entire themed lands may be responsible for several hundred attractions hosts and many complex attractions. Area managers are in constant contact with lead attractions hosts, maintenance teams, public safety teams, and custodial workers. Area managers may or may not be in charge of foodservice operations, which are often a completely separate department within the park.

To become an area manager you first have to become a very capable attractions host. Just as some people are not cut out for customer service, some people are not good at being in charge of other people. Being the boss seems prestigious, and the paycheck is certainly bigger, but bosses have to be willing to take responsibility for other people and the decisions they make. An area manager will not get fired if an attractions host makes a big mistake. If there are many big mistakes in the same area, senior management will come to the conclusion that the area manager is not doing a very good job.

Attraction Designer

Attraction designers are the gifted creative pros who dream up the attractions that make theme parks so much fun. It is hard to clearly define attraction designers because they come from such a wide array of backgrounds. The first attractions at Disneyland, for example, were designed by animators from Disney's film studio because they happened to be on the payroll when

Walt Disney needed some help to bring his vision to life.

Some attraction designers, like those first Disneyland designers, are artists, first and foremost. They dream up experiences and create impressive visual elements to go with them. They can be painters, graphic designers, sculptors and even writers. They create the vision that forms the basis of the attraction. Dark rides – rides that take guests on a guided journey through a darkened attraction – are long on artistic vision.

Other attraction designers are engineers. Industrial and mechanical engineers are the most common in the theme park business, but electrical engineers and industrial designers – a sort of cross between an engineer and an artist – are also in this work. Some attractions demand the skills of an engineer, like roller coasters that hurtle guests at great speeds. Such attractions also get artistic treatment, like painting, landscaping and branding to go with the engineering prowess.

Ultimately, all attractions require the skills of both artists and engineers. Dark rides need ride vehicles to ferry guests through imaginary scenarios, while roller coasters often come with elaborate themes that can only be created by artists. There is no automatic path to a career as an attraction designer. Assess your talents, develop your skills and do everything you can to apply them to the theme park business.

Theme Park Manager

To say that theme park managers have tremendous responsibility is putting it mildly. The manager of a theme park, the boss in charge of everything, has to have a solid understanding of attractions, foodservice, custodial matters, health and safety, retailing, labor laws, live shows and parades, and innumerable rules and regulations imposed by local authorities. In most industries, senior managers have to keep track of people and operations within a fairly narrow range. This is not so for theme park managers.

Theme park managers almost always come up through the ranks. There just is no other way to learn everything they need to know. Many theme park managers earn degrees along the way, in subjects like business administration, management, communications, or parks and recreation. They may also have earned degrees in the arts or engineering, depending upon the exact path they took to get to the top.

Nobody succeeds in this business by staying on a narrow career path. Theme park managers are the cast members who always stepped up for hard jobs, who were always willing to try something new. They volunteered for overtime, earned degrees and professional certificates that set them apart from the crowd, and made everybody who worked with them better for it. If your goal is to make it to the top, you need to be the kind of person who will eagerly tackle any task.

Theme park managers are also the link between the theme park operators and corporate executives who run the company that owns the theme park. Theme park managers are expected to report to top brass on a regular basis, filing reports, submitting recommendations, and making presentations. They need to know how to deal with corporate accountants, lawyers, and public relations professionals. Some theme park managers make the leap from working in the park to working in the head office. This is a decision you can only make when you get there. Many theme park people get into the business because they do not want to work in a desk job in a normal office. You may be surprised at where you want to go later in life, when you have a family and other responsibilities.

STORIES OF PEOPLE IN THEME PARK CAREERS

I Am a Roller Coaster Designer

"When I was a kid I begged my parents to take the family on vacations to theme parks so I could ride roller coasters. I joined American Coaster Enthusiasts when I was 16 and have been a member ever since. I worked summers at a theme park near my home when I was in high school, and then went to college in a part of the country where I could work part time at theme parks year-round while I went to school. I majored in structural engineering and took as many courses as I could in mechanical engineering. That's the formula for a coaster-crazed kid.

Roller coaster technology has grown by leaps and bounds in the last few decades. The great coasters of the past were enormous wooden structures that depended upon steep hills and graceful curves for their thrills. There are still many of them in existence, and coaster fans love them for their old-school design and rickety ride quality that is always a little alarming. The creaking and groaning of the wood, along with the clickety-clack of the tracks and the rushing wind makes wooden coasters incredibly loud and visceral in a way that modern steel coasters just aren't. Love 'em.

But modern steel coasters can do things that wooden coasters just can't. They can go upside down, do corkscrews, tumble through negative angles, be thrust forward by magnetic launch systems, and go much,

much faster than their wooden forebears could ever dream of. They are what today's coaster enthusiasts demand, and it's my job to give it to them.

Computers are the secret to modern coaster design. With computers we can build simulations and test out ideas in digits before we spend serious money on them. Computer aided design applications – CAD – also allow us to design and manufacture incredibly complex parts to very close tolerances. A twisting, turning coaster requires thousands of parts that aren't quite identical. The next part in the track is always just a fraction of a degree different from the one that came before it. Before CAD it was just too hard to design with that kind of precision.

Roller coasters are the epitome of engineer-led theme park attractions. If artists designed coasters, people might be injured, but a coaster without art would be a boring mass of metal. Artists give coasters the flair and image that attracts guests to them in the first place. It's no coincidence that many of the most successful coasters of recent years were based on superhero themes. We engineers had to work with artists from the beginning to make sure we were designing a coaster that was in keeping with the theme. Even coasters not attached to an existing storyline have pretty aggressive branding. Coasters get names like Demon, Tidal Wave, Abyss, Boomerang, Pandemonium and Screamin' Eagle. Engineers give coasters their thrills, but artists give them their flair. It's an essential relationship."

I Am an Area Manager

"Like pretty much everybody in my position, I got my start in this business as an attractions host. Part time in high school and college, full time after graduation. I didn't really intend to stay in the theme park business. When I graduated from college with a bachelor's degree in business administration and management my part-time employer offered me an opportunity to go through their world-famous management training program and become a full-time manager. Why not?

I don't think anybody could go through the management training here without being an attractions host first. There's just so much to know about park operations and customer service that can only be learned on the front lines, that I don't think anybody from outside the business would even get it. By the time you get to management training, the company assumes you already know all of that. It's time for the next step.

The first thing you learn in management training is that you lead people and manage projects. There's a difference. Projects have many steps and phases that need to be managed. There are software applications to help you create spreadsheets and flowcharts to manage projects effectively. People have to be led carefully and tactfully. Most people don't respond well to blunt instructions. They want to know how their efforts fit into the larger project and they look to leaders to keep them informed. Leaders have to keep their subordinates enthused and all pulling in the same direction. Management training was a real eye opener for me.

As an area manager I am in charge of an entire themed

land. There are also managers in charge of foodservice, attractions, custodial services, retailing, maintenance and live performances. They all report to me. There are several thousand cast members in our land, working in all areas. Some are part-timers, some are full-timers. We schedule them all. The payroll just for our area is bigger than that of most companies. I am ultimately responsible for making sure that everything works together and that everybody who works here is happy and gainfully employed.

To illustrate just how varied and complex my job is, let me tell you about my morning. The first thing I do is walk through my area. I greet hosts, drop by the restaurants, check out the shelves in the stores, chat with the maintenance crews and generally get a grip on the day to come. When I get to my office there is almost always somebody waiting for me. Today it was the area foodservice manager who wanted to tell me about some supply problems that were going to cause problems during the lunch rush. After that it was the attractions manager, whose hair was on fire because the roller coaster in our area wasn't going to open on time due to a maintenance glitch. Then the maintenance chief gave me a rundown of the previous night's routine. After that, I answered a few emails from my boss, the park manager, who had a meeting with senior corporate executives that afternoon and needed some information. This was all before lunch, mind you.

I love this business. It's fast-paced and complicated, and some days are just plain hard, but I wouldn't trade it for anything. If I'm having a bad day I just step outside my office for a few minutes and take a stroll around the park. It only takes a minute to remind myself why I got into theme parks. There's no business like it. It really is magical."

I Am an Attractions Host

"I've always loved theme parks. I'm only in high school, and most of my friends have part-time jobs in fast-food restaurants. Nothing wrong with that, but with a major theme park nearby it never occurred to me to flip burgers. I wanted to get paid to work in a magical place.

Being an attractions host is fun right up until it's not. Let me explain. Most of the day my job is to help happy people have a good time. They've paid a lot of money to come to the park and they always walk through the main gate with a smile. My job is to keep them smiling. I help them on and off attractions, I give them directions to restrooms and eateries, and I tell corny jokes while they're standing in line. It's fun for them, and for me.

Except when it's not. Some days the park is extra-crowded. Lines are long, nerves are frayed and people's expectations aren't being met because they are spending more time in line than they are enjoying themselves. Add high temperatures or heavy rain and you have a recipe for disgruntled guests. That's when the job gets hard. I've been yelled at by unhappy guests more times than I can count. I was even pushed around by one guest and had to call security to have her thrown out. I have had some of the world's best training in customer service, and I take pride in my ability to keep guests happy, but I won't kid you, some days are a real challenge.

I don't know if I want to make theme parks a career.

There is no doubt that I've learned a lot in this job. My customer service skills are top-notch, and I can keep my cool in the face of just about anything. I can see how people are attracted to the theme park business as a career. It's so complex and there are so many people here doing amazing things. Do I want to make it my long-term career? I have a few years to think about it."

I Design Dark Rides

"I didn't intend to design dark rides. It just happened. By training, I am an artist. A painter, mostly, but I also dabble in sculpture and graphic design. I was hired to be an animator in the movie studio owned by my company. When the boss got this crazy idea to build a theme park he started by rounding up some of the studio artists and asking us to help flesh out the ideas.

We started by turning the boss's sketches into detailed drawings. Then we kicked them around with studio writers so they told a story. Along the way we built models, made more drawings and elaborated upon the original ideas. The boss came by regularly to weigh in on our work.

We literally had to invent things to make our ideas come to life. Our company holds many of the earliest patents on robotics, for example. The newest thing is augmented reality using special goggles. We also still use old-fashioned trickery to create special effects for some attractions. One of the most effective was Pepper's Ghost, an age-old mirror trick that still looks good today.

Working with mechanical engineers to invent robots was definitely not what I had in mind when I signed on with the movie studio, but it was a fascinating twist that made my career better than I had hoped for. Although I came from the artist side of the house, I learned a lot by working with the engineers who helped to bring our ideas to life. They are the other part of the equation. We couldn't do it without them. Our goals are the same, but we take different paths to get there.

Here's a great story about why it's so important for artists and engineers to work together on attractions. Some years ago I designed a tower for a theme park. It wasn't a ride. It was a tall, complex tower with whirlygigs and propellers and such, and it was all linked together by a light and airy tubular structure. I handed the design off to the engineers and thought it was a done deal. When I saw the finished product a few months later I was horrified. My light and airy tubular structure had been turned into a thick, heavy armature that was not at all what I had in mind. The engineers told me that my original design was too light, and never would have stood up to strong winds. If I'd known that I would have designed it differently!"

PERSONAL QUALIFICATIONS

TO SUCCEED IN THIS BUSINESS YOU MUST have exceptional customer service skills. Customer service is the lifeblood of the theme park business. As Walt Disney noted, old-fashioned amusement parks were known for their roughness and lack of customer service. Guests at modern theme parks demand excellent customer service every minute of every day. A busy summer weekend can be a nightmare in a theme park. Lines are long, kids are cranky, and tempers flare when the weather gets hot. Excellent customer service is what keeps everything from boiling over. Theme park admission is also expensive, and guests have every right to demand that they be treated well when they walk through the gates. Anybody who aspires to a career dealing directly with customers' needs to have a flair for customer service. While some customer service skills can be taught, the happiest workers already have the patience and empathy needed to be successful.

Logistics is also important in the theme park business. The typical theme park crams an incredible amount of activity into a very small space. For example, 50,000 people may visit a theme park on a busy day. Most of them will arrive by automobile, which means there need to be about 15,000 parking spaces and an efficient means of directing traffic into them. Then, all the visitors have to get through a relatively small entrance and into the park. Keeping everybody moving is essential to avoid overcrowding. Walt Disney solved this problem by putting what he called "a weenie at the end of every street." There was always something in the distance to draw guests onward and keep them moving. Once in the park, guests have to be drawn into attractions, which means getting them to stand in queues. Queues have to move as quickly as possible in order to prevent problems, which is why many queues have pre-show attractions like videos to keep guests entertained while they are waiting in line. Fifty-thousand guests could easily eat more than 100,000 meals and countless snacks in a single day. All of that food has to be trucked into the park, in a way that does not ruin the view or inconvenience the guests. Then it all has to be distributed around the park, cooked and served. Merchandise also has to get into the park's shops, and stocked and displayed. At the end of the day, all of those people need to be gently ushered out of the park (which is why end-of-day parades always start at the back of the park and work their way toward the front, taking the guests with them). Maintenance generally takes place overnight, when the park is empty and attractions can be shut down for a few hours. When this process goes well it is like a logistical ballet. When it goes poorly everything falls apart.

The theme park business is about having fun. A whimsical nature is a bonus in this business, partly for the reason that whimsy is the driving theme behind most theme parks. Fairy-tale princesses, talking animals and comic-book superheroes are not reality. If you think putting on a costume to look like a giant chipmunk is ridiculous, you probably should not be in the theme park business.

ATTRACTIVE FEATURES

GETTING PAID TO DO SOMETHING YOU LOVE is always a sweet deal. Making a living in the theme park business comes very close to getting paid to do something you would happily do for free. You will not be paid to spend all day hanging out in the park and having fun like a guest, but working in a theme park comes pretty close. Theme parks work their magic by creating immersive environments in which guests can imagine that they are far away from the real world and the stresses that come with it. They can spend a day or two in a medieval village, a jungle safari, a vision of the future, or a world filled with superheroes. Theme park cast members get to spend their days there, every day. Managers and designers create these magical places and keep them up and running.

Modern theme parks are incredibly complex operations offering careerists almost limitless opportunities to expand their horizons while they pursue their careers. It is quite common for theme park professionals to start out working in the park in attractions, custodial, maintenance, transportation or foodservice. From there, they become managers of groups of attractions, areas, restaurants or other operations. Then they graduate to behind-the-scenes positions making decisions about what happens on stage. Along the way they may switch jobs several times, learning about different operations within the park and its associated operations, like hotels. There may be opportunities for professional education along the way. If you pursue a career in the theme park business you will never be bored.

People go to theme parks for rejuvenation, to get a little lift out of their daily routine. They want to laugh and scream and eat fun food. Theme park professionals give them what they want.

UNATTRACTIVE ASPECTS

THE THEME PARK BUSINESS IS NOT ALL about working in a magical environment and making people happy. The theme park business employs several hundred thousand people in the United States alone. The majority of those employees are hourly cast members staffing the attractions and restaurants in the parks. Some are salaried managers who run the parks and make the day-to-day decisions that keep the parks running. Just a few become the designers and engineers who dream it all up. Not surprisingly, hourly cast members tend to be young people with few expenses or older people retired from something else and looking for a fun job to add structure to their lives. Managers earn moderate incomes. Only a very small percentage of theme park professionals earn high salaries, usually as senior managers or in backstage positions like designers and engineers. Earning a living in the theme park business is a wonderful way to spend your working years, but it is unlikely to make you rich.

All leisure industries are susceptible to ups and downs in the economy. People cut back on optional spending when times are tough. As much as you may love theme parks, they are not a basic necessity. Economic downturns often lead to layoffs in the theme park business, especially among the large number of hourly employees who do most of the day-to-day work.

EDUCATION AND TRAINING

THERE IS NO FORMAL EDUCATIONAL REQUIREMENT to enter the theme park business. You owe it to yourself to pursue a bachelor's degree, however, both to learn advanced skills and to make yourself stand out from the crowd of mostly young, hourly cast members who may or may not plan to make theme parks a career. You need to be able to show potential employers that you are in it for the long haul.

The theme park business employs so many people in so many different professions that you should feel free to major in whatever you want, and then apply that knowledge to a career in theme parks. Want to design rides and attractions? Major in engineering or industrial design, or graphic arts and design. Want to manage areas or even entire parks? Major in business administration and management. Want to pursue the performing arts within the theme park business? Major in the performing arts – drama, dance, music. Have a flair for food? Major in culinary arts.

Any of these paths can get your foot in the door in the theme park business. They will also set you up for continuing success in a succession of fun and interesting jobs. If your goal is to design or manage theme parks, however, you should pursue an education that specifically targets your long-term goal. If your goal is to design theme parks you can earn a degree in engineering or industrial design. Architecture and urban planning are also good choices. If you want to manage theme parks you should definitely stick to business administration and management. In either case, you should feel free to fine tune your educational pursuits to align with your own interests and opportunities.

There is one degree option that you should seriously consider. Many universities offer degrees in parks and recreation, often with concentrations in subjects like travel and tourism, sports management, park and recreation area management, and golf management. Many programs also offer opportunities to take classes in related fields like culinary arts and restaurant management, recreation and physical therapy, and business administration and management. Demand for graduates with degrees in parks and recreation has grown rapidly in recent years as people take more time for leisure pursuits.

No matter what path you choose to take for your education you will have to make it clear to potential employers that your goal is to establish a long-term career in the theme park business. If you live near a theme park – or a business with some similarities, like a standalone theme attraction, golf course or vacation resort, for example – make an effort to get a part-time job there while you pursue your studies. You will be able to apply what you learn right away and set yourself up for a full-time job after graduation.

The best way to get some real-world experience while you pursue your degree is to complete an internship. Many theme parks offer internship programs. They are especially common at northern theme parks that are only open during the summer. These parks often hire thousands of workers for a few months, and may offer housing and transportation, too.

There is one internship program you should seriously consider: the Disney College Program. Offering internships at both Walt Disney World in Florida and at Disneyland Resort in California, the Disney College Program has given innumerable aspiring theme park careerists the best start they could ask for. Thousands of college students from around the world apply annually for a spot in one of the three programs offered each year. Each program lasts for one semester, and students who complete the spring program can apply to stay on for the busy summer season. To apply, students must be at least 18 years old and currently enrolled in a college or university program or be no more than 12 months past graduation. Candidates must also meet whatever criteria their schools require for internships, such as achieving a minimum grade-point average, pursuing an acceptable major or agreeing to complete an assignment during their internship, like a paper or other project. Not all applicants are accepted into the program the first time they apply, and it is not uncommon for candidates to apply more than once. Students accepted into the program report to Florida or California where they are assigned a job in a theme park, hotel or restaurant – depending upon their major, interest or prior experience – and are provided with housing and transportation to get to and from work. Students then take a series of classes designed to turn them into cast members. The program also comes with weekly seminars exploring various parts of Disney's business, including lessons on customer service, company history and leadership. Check out the careers page on the Disney website for more information.

EARNINGS

MOST THEME PARK WORKERS EARN MODEST to moderate salaries. Theme park jobs typically start out at or near the minimum wage. This is especially true for northern theme parks that are only open during the summer months. These parks need a small army of high school and college kids for a few months each year, and only need a handful of serious professionals to run the show. Year-round theme parks, like those in the epicenters of Central Florida and Southern California, tend to pay better and come with better benefits. These parks have an interest in nurturing professionals who will stay for the long haul. Entry-level jobs may still start at or near the minimum wage, but there will be no lack of opportunities to move up in the world.

Generally speaking, theme parks promote the best hourly employees into salaried positions based on their demonstrated customer service skills and mastery of their jobs. Often, these frontrunners are recruited for in-house management training programs in which they learn the essential skills required to manage projects and lead people. Successful graduates of management training programs are typically put on a salary and assigned a job that comes with supervisory responsibilities. These positions can start at $50,000 to $60,000 per year, and tend to rise over time.

Not all theme park careerists work for theme parks. Many of the designers and engineers who create attractions actually work for independent companies which are hired by theme parks for specific projects. Earnings for these professionals are hard to pin down, but structural engineers with advanced degrees and experience can easily earn more than $100,000 per year. The same goes for designers with strong track records. Entrepreneurs who start businesses providing advanced services can conceivably make millions.

A few in-house theme park experts achieve high salaries. The Walt Disney Company maintains an entire division devoted to theme park design and engineering called Walt Disney Imagineering. Only the very best and brightest theme park professionals grow up to become Imagineers. The hardworking and highly creative few who make it to the top are very well compensated.

OPPORTUNITIES

AFTER YOU START YOUR CAREER in theme parks, you will probably want to climb the ladder as quickly as possible. Luckily, there are plenty of ways to do it. Keep an eye on internal job postings and never be afraid to try something new. Modern theme parks employ careerists in many different fields. Most careerists start out as an attractions host, which is the easiest way to get into the business and also an essential step in learning about how to provide excellent customer service. Serious theme park professionals do not stay at this level for very long, however. They seek out opportunities to learn as much as they can about the business. This means keeping an eye on job opportunities with your current employer. Do you qualify for a management training program? Are you interested in trying your hand in a different part of the park, or in a completely different position? Senior managers have to understand how all of the park's major functions work, and how they work together. The only way to gain such knowledge is to spread yourself around. If you run out of opportunities with your current employer, look further afield.

Some theme park jobs require professional certifications. This is especially true for the most thrilling attractions, which may require hosts to pass examinations to prove that they know how to run the attraction safely. Culinary careerists have to earn the same public health certificates any other restaurant employees have to earn. Universities in areas with many theme parks often offer professional certificates in subjects important to the theme park business, like personnel management in the hospitality business.

Perhaps the best advice is doing everything you can to stand out from your peers, especially early in your career. The theme park business employs many people who are only in it for a little while. They may enjoy it, but they have other plans for their future. You are different and you need to make sure everybody knows it.

GETTING STARTED

GETTING YOUR FIRST JOB AFTER COLLEGE should not be too hard, as long as you follow a few simple rules. Get your personal marketing materials together. A well-written résumé is critical to your job search. Most résumés are scrutinized by potential employers for about 10 seconds, so you owe it to yourself to write a solid résumé that will make an impact. Your college or university may have a placement office that can help you put together a winning résumé, and there is certainly no shortage of books and software applications that can help you to prepare one yourself. A traditional résumé that can be printed out and easily read is essential.

Send your résumé to everybody you know in the theme park business. Send it to every boss you have ever had, teachers who may have a few connections, and anybody else you can think of who may be able to point you in the right direction. Many careerists get their first jobs after college with the companies with whom they completed their internships. Many others land a job by networking, networking, networking.

Do not get wrapped around a specific idea of the perfect job. You do not know what your dream job is yet. You will be amazed at how much you will learn during the first few years of your career. Do not be afraid to take the first good opportunity that comes along. The theme park business is so varied and complex that you will have no problem weaving through the endless opportunities and seizing the ones that are right for you. A few years down the road you may be somewhere you never dreamed of.

ASSOCIATIONS, PERIODICALS, WEBSITES

■ **All Ears**
www.allears.net

■ **American Coaster Enthusiasts**
www.aceonline.org

■ **American Society of Civil Engineers**
www.asce.org

■ **American Society of Mechanical Engineers**
www.asme.org

- **Attractions Magazine**
  www.attractionsmagazine.com

- **Behind the Thrills**
  www.behindthethrills.com

- **Cedar Fair**
  www.cedarfair.com

- **Chip and Co.**
  www.chipandco.com

- **Coaster 101**
  www.coaster101.com

- **Coaster Critic**
  www.coastercritic.com

- **Coaster Radio**
  www.coasterradio.com

- **Disney Food Blog**
  www.disneyfoodblog.com

- **Disney Tourist Blog**
  www.disneytouristblog.com

- **Doombuggies**
  www.doombuggies.com

- **Mice Chat**
  www.micechat.com

- **Orlando Informer**
  www.orlandoinformer.com

- **Orlando Parks News**
  www.orlandoparksnews.com

- **Orlando Parkstop**
  www.orlandoparkstop.com

- **Parkeology**
www.parkeology.com

- **Rolly Crump**
www.rolandcrump.com

- **Sea World**
www.seaworld.com

- **Six Flags**
www.sixflags.com

- **Structural Engineers Association of Southern California**
www.seaosc.org

- **Tell No Tales**
www.tellnotales.com

- **The Walt Disney Company**
www.disney.com

- **Theme Park Hipster**
www.themeparkhipster.com

- **Theme Park Insider**
www.themeparkinsider.com

- **Theme Park Trader**
www.themeparktrader.com

- **Theme Park University**
www.themeparkuniversity.com

- **Universal Studios**
www.universalstudios.com

- **Walt Disney Imagineering**
www.disneyimaginations.com

Copyright 2019   Institute For Career Research
CAREERS INTERNET DATABASE
www.careers-internet.org

www.ingramcontent.com/pod-product-compliance
Lightning Source LLC
Chambersburg PA
CBHW072310170526
45158CB00003BA/1262